FRIENDS FOR FREEDOM

*"Forget what the world will say . . . ;
think your best thoughts, speak your
best words, do your best works."*

—Susan B. Anthony

*"I would unite with anybody to do right
and with nobody to do wrong."*

—Frederick Douglass

FRIENDS FOR

THE STORY OF SUSAN B. ANTHONY & FREDERICK DOUGLASS

Suzanne Slade

Illustrated by Nicole Tadgell

FREEDOM

Charlesbridge

With love to Georganne, my sister and close friend—S. S.
For Lara—N. T.

Special thanks to Dr. C. James Trotman, Professor Emeritus of English and Founding Director of the Frederick Douglass Institute at West Chester University and author of *Frederick Douglass: A Biography*, and Ellen Wheeler, Public Relations and Communications Director at the National Susan B. Anthony Museum & House, for their invaluable expertise and advice.

Text copyright © 2014 by Suzanne Slade
Illustrations copyright © 2014 by Nicole Tadgell

Published by Charlesbridge
85 Main Street
Watertown, MA 02472
(617) 926-0329
www.charlesbridge.com

Library of Congress Cataloging-in-Publication Data
Slade, Suzanne.
   Friends for freedom: the story of Susan B. Anthony & Frederick Douglass/Suzanne Slade; illustrated by Nicole Tadgell.
      pages cm
   ISBN 978-1-58089-568-2 (reinforced for library use)
   ISBN 978-1-60734-749-1 (ebook)
   ISBN 978-1-60734-651-7 (ebook pdf)
   1. Anthony, Susan B. (Susan Brownell), 1820–1906—Juvenile literature. 2. Douglass, Frederick, 1818–1895—Juvenile literature. 3. Suffragists—United States—Biography—Juvenile literature. 4. Abolitionists—United States—Biography—Juvenile literature. 5. Social reformers—United States—Biography—Juvenile literature. I. Title.
HQ1413.A55S538 2014
303.48'40922—dc23
[B]   2013022795

Printed in Singapore
(hc) 10 9 8 7 6 5 4 3 2 1

Illustrations painted on Fabriano Artistico 140-lb. bright-white cold-press paper with
   Winsor & Newton watercolors
Display type set in Poplar and text type set in Monotype Baskerville
Color separations by KHL Chroma Graphics, Singapore
Printed and bound February 2014 by Imago in Singapore
Production supervision by Brian G. Walker
Designed by Susan Mallory Sherman

No one thought Susan and Frederick would become friends.

Susan B. Anthony was born in a two-story home with polished wood floors.

Frederick Douglass was born in a one-room cabin with floors made of clay.

Susan's parents taught her to read before she started school.

Frederick secretly taught himself to read because slaves weren't allowed to go to school.

Susan spent her days helping her mother—baking, sewing, and gardening.

Frederick spent his days obeying his master—chopping, plowing, and planting.

When Susan and Frederick were growing up, America was growing up, too. And this young country had some strange ideas about friendship.

It wasn't proper for women to be friends with men.

You weren't supposed to be friends with someone whose skin was a different color than yours.

But Susan and Frederick knew these ideas were wrong.

And when they grew up, they helped America grow up, too.

Their story began in the fall of 1849, when Susan quit teaching and moved home to the family farm near Rochester, New York. Before she even unpacked her bags, Susan hopped back into the wagon, grabbed the reins from her father, and drove those horses straight into town.

She couldn't wait to meet the man her father talked so much about—the man who made a daring escape from slavery, gave eloquent speeches about equality, and stood up for women.

When Frederick found Susan at his door, his smile lit up all of Alexander Street.

He'd heard quite a bit about her, too—the brave woman who gave powerful speeches about equality. The woman who wasn't afraid to complain that male teachers were paid four times more than women to do the same job.

Before you could say "liberty and justice for all," Frederick invited Susan inside and brewed up a pot of his finest tea.

As the tea cooled down, their conversation heated up. They both hated slavery and thought one person should never own another. They believed women deserved the same rights as men—to own land, go to college, and vote.

And they weren't afraid to stand up for their beliefs. In fact, they loved a good fight!

So the two became friends and decided to fight for equal rights for African Americans and women—together.

But would this odd friendship last?

Their friendship lasted when others laughed.

People pointed and made fun of Susan and Frederick when they went out together.

Whites and blacks weren't supposed to be friends! It just wasn't right for a black man and a white woman to be seen together in public.

But Susan and Frederick didn't care what others said, behind their backs or to their faces.

They were friends, no matter what.

Their friendship lasted when rotten eggs flew.

Susan and Frederick visited nearby towns to share their ideas.

"Everyone deserves to be treated the same!" they declared.

But they met lots of enemies—people willing to do anything to stop them.

Reporters wrote nasty stories saying that Susan and Frederick were like a terrible sickness. "A deadly smallpox! A horrible plague!"

Angry crowds pelted them with rotten eggs. "You two are crazy, and your ideas are crazy, too!"

But nothing could stop the two friends.

Their friendship lasted when danger drew near.

In 1861 Susan and Frederick headed to New York's capital, Albany, to speak out against slavery.

More than one hundred people signed a petition to keep them out of the city. "Those radicals will cause riots!" they cried. "They'll embarrass our fine town."

But the two came anyway, and they brought more speakers with them.

That day the meeting hall was packed. Most people weren't there to listen. They'd come to scare the unwelcome visitors away.

"I don't want any trouble," the mayor announced, placing a gun on his lap for all to see.

Susan and Frederick bravely faced the loud, angry mob. Bloody brawls and fistfights broke out around them.

Through it all, the two friends kept speaking.

Their friendship lasted when tempers flared.

Four years later the Thirteenth Amendment finally ended
slavery. Susan and Frederick celebrated, then got right
back to work.

In 1869 newspaper headlines shocked the nation: the newly
proposed Fifteenth Amendment could give black men the right
to vote—but not women.

The country was in an uproar. Everyone took sides.

Frederick was thrilled.

Susan was furious.

They got into a fight—a real whopper!

"With us, the matter is a question of life and death,"
Frederick insisted.

"Women must stand back and wait?" Susan cried.

They argued and shouted. Worse yet—they fought in public
with everyone watching.

But Susan and Frederick kept listening to one another. In time, they realized they could disagree and still be friends. So they stopped fighting each other and were soon fighting side by side again.

Their friendship lasted when fires burned.

In 1872 hungry flames devoured Frederick's house while he was away on business. It was started by arsonists who didn't want African Americans in their town.

The blaze destroyed nearly everything—books, furniture, and even farm animals. Frederick's wife and children barely escaped with their lives.

When Frederick rushed back to Rochester, he found his family homeless. Standing beside charred bricks and ashes, he decided to move to Washington, DC, to fight for equality where the laws were made.

"Stay," Susan pleaded, hoping he'd rebuild in the town they'd shared for over twenty years. But Frederick's mind was made up. So the two friends said good-bye and promised to stay close.

Their friendship lasted when they were apart.

Separated by hundreds of miles, Susan and Frederick wrote each other long letters.

"My dear old friend," Susan's notes began.

"Yours for the freedom of man and woman always," Frederick wrote back.

They read about each other in newspapers.

They bounced down rocky roads to give speeches together.

They chugged across states to see one another at conventions.

And their friendship stayed as strong as ever.

Their friendship lasted over forty-five years!

Through good times and bad, Susan and Frederick remained friends. Together they saw many of their dreams come true.

African American men proudly stood in voting lines.

Women packed their bags and headed off to college.

African Americans and women worked jobs that were once only for white men.

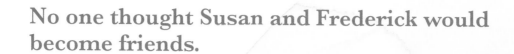

No one thought Susan and Frederick would become friends.

But it's a good thing they did.

Because when they grew up, they shared a lasting friendship—one that helped America grow up, too!

Author's Note

Susan and Frederick's friendship surprised many people and survived many challenges. But through it all the two remained friends because of their respect for each other and their shared belief that everyone deserves the same rights.

Like most friends, Susan and Frederick enjoyed working together, but they were also busy with their own projects. Each started a newspaper to promote equal rights. Both were excellent speakers who traveled across the country, sharing messages of equality.

Susan and Frederick often faced opposition when they gave speeches. In 1861 Susan organized the "No Compromise with Slaveholders" speaking tour, which traveled around New York. Frederick joined the tour in Albany, along with civil rights leaders Elizabeth Cady Stanton, Lucretia Mott, Martha Wright, and Gerrit Smith. Albany's mayor placed a revolver in his lap and warned the crowd that plainclothes policemen were stationed around the hall. But the mob paid no attention, and Susan and Frederick found themselves in danger again.

Although many people ridiculed Susan and Frederick, others strongly believed in the determined pair. In 1865 a well-known New York newspaper, the *Rochester Union and Advertiser*, published an article titled "The Winning Ticket," which supported Susan and Frederick: "We shall expect to see Mr. Douglas [*sic*] President and Miss Anthony Vice President of the United States. They would make a strong ticket."

Susan and Frederick's last day together was February 20, 1895, at a women's rights meeting in Washington, DC. Arm in arm, the two friends proudly walked onstage to a standing ovation. Sitting beside each other, they enjoyed one another's company all afternoon. That night Frederick had a heart attack and died in his home. A *New York Times* obituary noted important aspects of his life, including Susan: "Miss Anthony and Mr. Douglass formed an intimate friendship . . . , and that friendship had continued for many decades." A few days later Susan had to make one of the most difficult speeches of her life—a eulogy at Frederick's funeral—and say good-bye to her friend of forty-five years. Eleven years later Susan passed away at age eighty-six. But Susan and Frederick's dreams of equal rights didn't die. Their hard work continued to help shape future laws, including the Nineteenth Amendment, which finally gave women the right to vote in 1920.

Today a bronze sculpture in Rochester called *Let's Have Tea* features larger-than-life figures of Susan and Frederick sharing a pot of tea and warm conversation. Thousands of people visit the sculpture every year to remember these famous civil rights leaders and good friends.

Let's Have Tea by Pepsy M. Kettavong. Photo courtesy of Carol Bednar.

Author's Research Note

Years ago I wrote separate biographies about Susan B. Anthony and Frederick Douglass. During my research I learned of their remarkable friendship and wondered why I hadn't heard about it before. But uncovering details about that friendship turned out to be more challenging than I expected. My investigation introduced me to librarians in several states and to kind experts at the Susan B. Anthony Museum & House, the Chester County Historical Society, and the Frederick Douglass Institute. Their expertise and generosity were invaluable to this project, which took over three years to research.

The most elusive part of this story was when and where Susan and Frederick first met. One book claimed their first meeting was at the Anthonys' farmhouse outside Rochester, New York, where a civil rights group gathered on Sundays. Another said they met during Frederick's New York speaking tour in 1845. I reviewed Frederick's three autobiographies, but his books primarily focus on the years before he met Susan. Historians at the Susan B. Anthony Museum & House directed me to *The Life and Work of Susan B. Anthony* by Ida Husted Harper. This book, considered a primary source because it was written under Susan's guidance, says their historic meeting took place after Susan quit teaching at Canajoharie Academy and moved home to Rochester in fall 1849. While it's possible the two met earlier, *Friends for Freedom* reflects the 1849 date Susan indicated. Other well-documented dates support this time frame as well, such as the fact that Susan moved to Canajoharie, New York, in 1846 to teach, well before Frederick and his family moved to Rochester in 1847.

This story is based on true events, but I had to use my imagination to fill in details when no facts could be found. For example, when Susan and her father went to Frederick's house on Alexander Street, no one knows for sure who drove the buggy. I wondered if a young, determined Susan might have grabbed the reins and driven the horses those six miles into town. Similarly, there's no transcript of the angry crowds' rants or the mayor of Albany's warning, but the fictionalized dialogue conveys the sentiments found in my research. Susan and Frederick's fight over the Fifteenth Amendment on May 12, 1869, was recorded as part of a public debate, so their own words appear in the book. Also, many of their letters were carefully preserved, so the text contains the actual words they penned to one another.

During my investigation I discovered several touching facts that illustrate the bond Susan and her family shared with Frederick. The Anthonys sent a wagon into town many Sundays to bring Frederick's family out to their farmhouse to share a meal and visit. When Susan's father, Daniel, died in 1862, Frederick gave the eulogy at his dear friend's funeral. I found it especially moving that Frederick gave Susan a daguerreotype (black and white photo) of himself that she proudly displayed on her mantel alongside her treasured family photos. It might not seem unusual to give a picture to a friend, but back then, photographs were rare. People didn't own cameras, so a portrait could only be made in a studio with expensive equipment, which created a one-of-a-kind daguerreotype. This small gift was quite special, just like Susan and Frederick's friendship.

Illustrator's Note

Keeping the idea of friendship at the core of these illustrations is what really kept everything on track and together. Both Susan and Frederick are historical figures with a monumental status, and the seriousness of their causes is plain on their faces in photographs. But inside, they were regular people, with a solid, tender affection for one another.

Each friendship is a unique experience. Not all friendships last a lifetime, but if you're lucky enough to have a lifelong friend, you've got a true treasure.

Working on a historical book requires research, of course—something I really enjoy. Both the Susan B. Anthony Birthplace Museum and the Susan B. Anthony Museum & House were close enough to visit, and I was treated to seeing artifacts—including Susan's famous alligator purse—up close and personal. I very much appreciate the museum staff for spending time with me.

Very special thanks to Kay Demlow of Lavender's Green Historic Clothing for all her help with my questions about clothing of that time period. We have many photos of both Susan and Frederick, but alas, they are not in color. Kay's assistance was vital in helping me figure out what their clothes would have looked like from all sides—not just from the front, as we see in photographs.

Source Notes

p. 1: Susan B. Anthony (SBA): "Forget . . . best works": Sherr, p. 35.

Frederick Douglass (FD): "I would . . . wrong": Holland, p. 193.

p. 7: SBA was born in two-story home (Adams, MA): Harper, p. 12.

FD was born in one-room cabin (Tuckahoe, MD): Douglass, *The Life and Times of Frederick Douglass*, pp. 29, 31, 33.

SBA's family taught her to read beginning at age three: Harper, p. 14.

FD secretly taught himself to read: Douglass, *Narrative of the Life of Frederick Douglass*, pp. 37–39.

p. 10: SBA moved to Rochester in 1849 after leaving Canajoharie Academy: Harper, p. 55, and K. Anthony, p. 95.

SBA met FD in 1849: Harper, p. 60.

p. 12: FD's home was on Alexander Street: Susan B. Anthony House & Museum.

Male teachers were paid four times women's wages: Harper, p. 45.

p. 19: SBA and FD spoke in New York towns, were pelted with eggs: Burns and Ward, pp. 97, 98.

Reporters wrote nasty stories ("'Miss Susan B. Anthony & Co. were looked upon as a fatal species of small pox, London plague, or Montreal ship fever,' wrote one reporter"): Sherr, p. 30.

p. 21: SBA, FD, and others spoke in Albany as part of "No Compromise with Slaveholders" tour; over one hundred residents signed a petition to keep them out; mayor warned crowd and placed gun on lap; angry mob became violent: Harper, pp. 211–212.

p. 23: SBA and FD debated Fifteenth Amendment at American Equal Rights Association meeting, May 12, 1869: Sherr, pp. 39, 40.

FD: "I do not see how any one can pretend that there is the same urgency in giving the ballot to woman as to the negro. *With us, the matter is a question of life and death.*" (emphasis added)

SBA: "The question of precedence has no place on an equal rights platform. The only reason why it ever found a place here was that there were some who insisted that *woman must stand back and wait* until another class should be enfranchised." (emphasis added)

p. 24: SBA and FD reconciled after Fifteenth Amendment fight: Huggins, pp. 122, 159, Sherr, p. 31, and McFeely, p. 315.

p. 26: FD's house (1507 Pennsylvania Ave.) burned in 1872; FD was in Washington, DC, on business; fire destroyed books, furniture, and farm animals: McFeely, p. 272.

Fire was started by arsonist: McFeely, p. 275.

FD rejected SBA's request to rebuild in Rochester; FD moved family to Washington, DC: McFeely, pp. 275, 276.

p. 28: "My Dear Old Friend": SBA letter to FD (Feb. 6, 1888), the Frederick Douglass Papers.

"Yours for . . . man and woman always": FD letter to SBA, Harper, p. 215.

p. 29: FD gave SBA 1848 daguerreotype of himself (shown on desk): Burns and Ward, p. 33.

p. 30: SBA and FD shared close friendship until FD's death in 1895: Sherr, p. 29, Gordon, p. 85, and Harper, p. 60.

p. 34: Albany speakers: Harper, p. 212.

"We shall expect . . . strong ticket": From "Winning Ticket" article, Sherr, p. 44.

"Miss Anthony . . . many decades": "Death of Fred Douglass," p. 1.

SBA and FD walked onstage together, sat beside each other, at Feb. 20, 1895, meeting: "Death of Fred Douglass," p. 1.

Selected Bibliography

Anthony, Katharine. *Susan B. Anthony: Her Personal History and Her Era.* New York: Doubleday & Company, 1954.

Anthony, Susan B., and Ida Husted Harper, eds. *The History of Woman Suffrage.* Vol. 4. Reprint of the 1902 Hollenbeck Press edition, Project Gutenberg, 2009. www.gutenberg.org/files/29870/29870-h /29870-h.htm.

Burns, Ken, and Geoffrey C. Ward. *Not for Ourselves Alone: The Story of Elizabeth Cady Stanton and Susan B. Anthony.* New York: Alfred A. Knopf, 1999.

Chestnutt, Charles. *Frederick Douglass.* Boston: Small, Maynard and Co., 1899.

"Death of Fred Douglass." *The New York Times* (Feb. 21, 1895): 1. Accessed through ProQuest.

Dorr, Rheta Childe. *Susan B. Anthony.* New York: Frederick A. Stokes Co., 1928.

Douglass, Frederick. *The Life and Times of Frederick Douglass.* Hartford, CT: Park Publishing, 1882.

Douglass, Frederick. *Narrative of the Life of Frederick Douglass, an American Slave.* 1845. Reprinted with introduction by Henry Louis Gates, Jr. New York: Random House, 1997. Page references are to the 1997 edition.

The Frederick Douglass Papers. General Correspondence, 1888, Jan.–Feb. Library of Congress.

Gordon, Ann D., ed. *The Selected Papers of Elizabeth Cady Stanton and Susan B. Anthony.* Vol. 1, *In the School of Anti-Slavery, 1840–1866.* New Brunswick, NJ: Rutgers University Press, 1997.

Harper, Ida Husted. *The Life and Work of Susan B. Anthony.* Vol. 1. Reprint of the 1899 Bowen-Merrill edition, Project Gutenberg, 2005. www.gutenberg.org/files/15220/15220-h /15220-h.htm.

Holland, Frederic May. *Frederick Douglass: The Colored Orator.* New York: Funk & Wagnalls, 1891. Accessed through Google Books. http://bit.ly/1bXnBWG.

Huggins, Nathan Irvin. *Slave and Citizen: The Life of Frederick Douglass.* Boston: Little, Brown and Co., 1980.

McFeely, William S. *Frederick Douglass.* Reprint ed. New York: W. W. Norton and Co., 1995.

Sherr, Lynn. *Failure Is Impossible: Susan B. Anthony in Her Own Words.* New York: Times Books, 1995.

Stanton, Elizabeth Cady, Susan B. Anthony, and Matilda Joslyn Gage, eds. *History of Woman Suffrage.* Vol. 1. Reprint of the 1889 edition, Project Gutenberg, 2009. www.gutenberg.org/files/28020/28020-h /28020-h.htm.

Stanton, Elizabeth Cady, Susan B. Anthony, and Matilda Joslyn Gage, eds. *History of Woman Suffrage.* Vol. 2. Reprint of the 1881 edition, Project Gutenberg, 2009. www.gutenberg.org/files/28039/28039-h /28039-h.htm.

Time Line

1818 Frederick Augustus Washington Bailey is born in Tuckahoe, Maryland. (Exact date unknown because slaves' birth records were not kept.)

1820 Susan Brownell Anthony is born February 15 in Adams, Massachusetts.

1838 Frederick escapes to New York, marries Anna Murray, and changes his name to Frederick Douglass in order to hide from slave hunters.

1845 Frederick finishes his first autobiography, *Narrative of the Life of Frederick Douglass, an American Slave.*

1846 Susan accepts a teaching position at Canajoharie Academy and moves to Canajoharie, New York. Frederick legally becomes a free person after British supporters buy his freedom from his former master.

1847 Frederick, his wife, Anna, and their four children move to Rochester, New York. Frederick starts an antislavery newspaper, *The North Star,* which also fights for the rights of women and other oppressed groups.

1849 Susan quits teaching and moves back to the family farm in Rochester. Susan and Frederick meet.

1850 Frederick and other antislavery activists dine at Susan's home most Sundays.

1855 Frederick releases his second autobiography, *My Bondage and My Freedom.*

1861 The Civil War begins. Susan organizes a "No Compromise with Slaveholders" antislavery tour in New York. During the tour Susan and Frederick speak to an unruly mob in Albany.

1862 Susan's father dies. Frederick gives the eulogy at his funeral.

1863 President Abraham Lincoln issues the Emancipation Proclamation on January 1.

1865 The Civil War ends. The Thirteenth Amendment passes, freeing all slaves in the United States.

1868 Susan and Elizabeth Cady Stanton start a newspaper called *The Revolution,* which supports equal rights for women and African Americans.

1869 Susan and Frederick publicly disagree over the Fifteenth Amendment at the American Equal Rights Association meeting on May 12.

1870 The Fifteenth Amendment is ratified, giving African American men the right to vote.

1872 Susan is arrested for voting. Frederick's Rochester home is burned down by arsonists. His family moves to Washington, DC.

1881 Frederick's third autobiography, *Life and Times of Frederick Douglass,* is published.

1884 Susan and Frederick speak out for women's rights at the first suffrage convention allowed in the Hall of the House of Representatives.

1895 Susan and Frederick attend a National Council of Women meeting in Washington, DC. That evening Frederick dies at home, age 77.

1897–98 Susan works with Ida Husted Harper to write her biography, *The Life and Work of Susan B. Anthony.*

1906 Susan dies at her home in Rochester, age 86.

1920 The Nineteenth Amendment is ratified on August 18, giving women the right to vote.